DISCOVERING THE ICEMAN

First published in Canada in 1996 by
Scholastic Canada Ltd.
123 Newkirk Road
Richmond Hill, Ontario L4C 3G5

Canadian Cataloguing in Publication Data

Tanaka, Shelley
Discovering the iceman: what was it like to find a 5,300-year-old mummy?

(I was there)
ISBN 0-590-24950-9 (bound) ISBN 0-590-24951-7 (pbk.)

1. Copper age — Italy — Trentino-Alto Adige — Juvenile literature.
2. Mummies — Italy — Trentino-Alto Adige — Juvenile literature.
3. Trentino-Alto Adige (Italy) — Antiquities — Juvenile literature.
I. McGaw, Laurie.   II. Title.   III. Series.

GN778.22.I8T35 1996   j937'.3   C96-930757-8

Design and Art Direction: Gordon Sibley Design Inc.
Maps and Diagrams: Jack McMaster
Editorial Director: Hugh M. Brewster
Project Editor: Nan Froman
Production Director: Susan Barrable
Production Co-ordinator: Donna Chong
Color Separation: Colour Technologies
Printing and Binding: Artegrafica S.p.A.

Discovering the Iceman was produced by Madison Press Books
which is under the direction of Albert E. Cummings.

Madison Press Books
40 Madison Avenue
Toronto, Ontario
Canada M5R 2S1

Endpapers: The Ötztal Alps, near the border of Austria and Italy, where the Iceman was discovered.
Previous page and right: The Iceman as he may have looked more than five thousand years ago.

Printed in Italy

DISCOVERING THE
ICEMAN

What was it like to find a 5,300-year-old mummy?

BY SHELLEY TANAKA, ILLUSTRATIONS BY LAURIE McGAW

Historical consultants

Janet E. Levy, Walter Leitner, Konrad Spindler

A SCHOLASTIC/MADISON PRESS BOOK

Part One

THE DISCOVERY

September 19, 1991

The sun was hot that day, the sky blue and clear. To Erika and Helmut Simon, the glistening white peaks of the Alps seemed to stretch forever.

Like thousands of other hikers, the Simons loved to climb the craggy slopes of this magnificent mountain range. Every morning they would pack a lunch and follow the mapped trails to one of the summits. Often they climbed the same narrow paths that shepherds used thousands of years ago to lead their sheep and goats up to the high mountain pastures.

Today the Simons' destination was the 11,535-foot (3,516-meter) peak known as the Finailspitze.

Erika and Helmut Simon stop for a picture during their climb on the day they discovered the Iceman.

They reached the summit just before noon and sat down to enjoy the spectacular view.

Later, on their way back down the mountain, they decided to leave the marked path. They wanted to take a shortcut back to the hut where they had left their backpacks. Crossing a glacier, the Simons made their way around a narrow hollow.

That's when they saw it.

It looked like a doll at first — a bare, brown head and bony shoulders sticking out of a slushy puddle of melting snow.

The Simons drew nearer. They bent down for a closer look.

"It's a man!" cried Erika.

Where was the Iceman found?

The Iceman was discovered in the Ötztal Alps, a mountain range that lies between Austria and Italy. His body was found just inside the Italian border.

GERMANY

AUSTRIA

Innsbruck •

SWITZERLAND

X Ötztal Alps

• Bolzano

ITALY

Venice •

ITALY

5

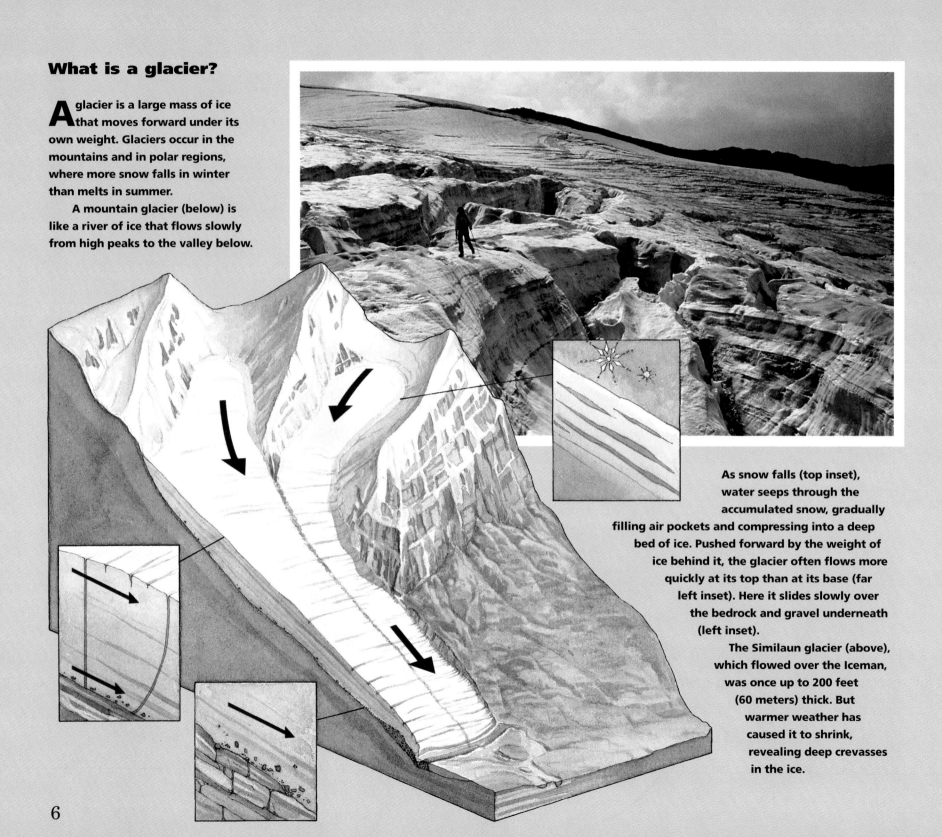

What is a glacier?

A glacier is a large mass of ice that moves forward under its own weight. Glaciers occur in the mountains and in polar regions, where more snow falls in winter than melts in summer.

A mountain glacier (below) is like a river of ice that flows slowly from high peaks to the valley below.

As snow falls (top inset), water seeps through the accumulated snow, gradually filling air pockets and compressing into a deep bed of ice. Pushed forward by the weight of ice behind it, the glacier often flows more quickly at its top than at its base (far left inset). Here it slides slowly over the bedrock and gravel underneath (left inset).

The Similaun glacier (above), which flowed over the Iceman, was once up to 200 feet (60 meters) thick. But warmer weather has caused it to shrink, revealing deep crevasses in the ice.

6

Two days later, on September 21, 1991, archeologist Konrad Spindler was getting ready for a new term of teaching and research at the University of Innsbruck in Austria. He was reading the local newspaper when he spotted a short item. Two tourists had found a body sticking out of a glacier in the Alps. The police had been called. They thought the corpse might belong to a mountain climber who had died in an accident, maybe several decades ago.

Spindler paid little attention. The body of a modern-day mountain climber didn't much interest an archeologist who specialized in ancient things. Besides, Spindler lived at the foot of the Alps, and he knew the mountains were a dangerous place. Rockslides, avalanches, crevasses, and sudden fogs or snow squalls could swallow up travelers in an instant. About two hundred hikers died in the Alps every year. The death of yet another mountain climber was sad, but it was not unusual.

So he was surprised to see that the body was still in the news a few days later. People had started to notice some odd things about this particular corpse. There were peculiar marks on the man's back. There was a big clump of straw on his foot, covered with torn pieces of leather. Strange tools lay scattered around him. A squashed birch-bark tube had been found nearby.

Beneath the glacier, the Iceman's body and clothing were preserved for thousands of years. But as soon as the ice melted and his clothing was exposed to the open air, much of it disintegrated and was blown away by the wind, leaving him almost naked.

And there were more mysteries. The body didn't look like the corpses that normally emerged from the glacier. It hadn't been crushed and torn apart by the grinding force of the ice. Its skin wasn't white and waxy but brown and shriveled like that of a mummy. It appeared to be quite old.

Rescue workers chip away at the ice surrounding the Iceman (top). Later, they place his body, a small dagger, and part of his bow in a body bag. A helicopter (middle) transports the find to a nearby town, where it is placed in a coffin (bottom).

Early in the morning of September 24, 1991, the phone rang in Spindler's office. It was the university's forensic department.

Spindler learned that air rescue operators and mountaineers had been hacking at the body for several days. Finally they were able to pull it out of the ice. It had been wrapped in a plastic bag, stuffed into a coffin, and taken to the nearest medical lab. At that very moment, it lay on a stainless-steel table — in a building that was only minutes away from Spindler's office. Would he like to see it?

It was very quiet and cool in the laboratory. The room smelled like a hospital. The forensic experts led Spindler to a dissecting table covered with a sheet. A clock ticked softly.

Spindler would remember this precise moment for the rest of his life. It was exactly 8:05 A.M.

The sheet was pulled away. And there lay the shriveled, naked body of a man.

His nose was squashed. His mouth was gaping. His eyelids were open, and sunken eyeballs gazed out of their sockets. His left hip had been torn open by a jackhammer that had been used to try to free him from the ice.

But what interested Spindler the most were the

8

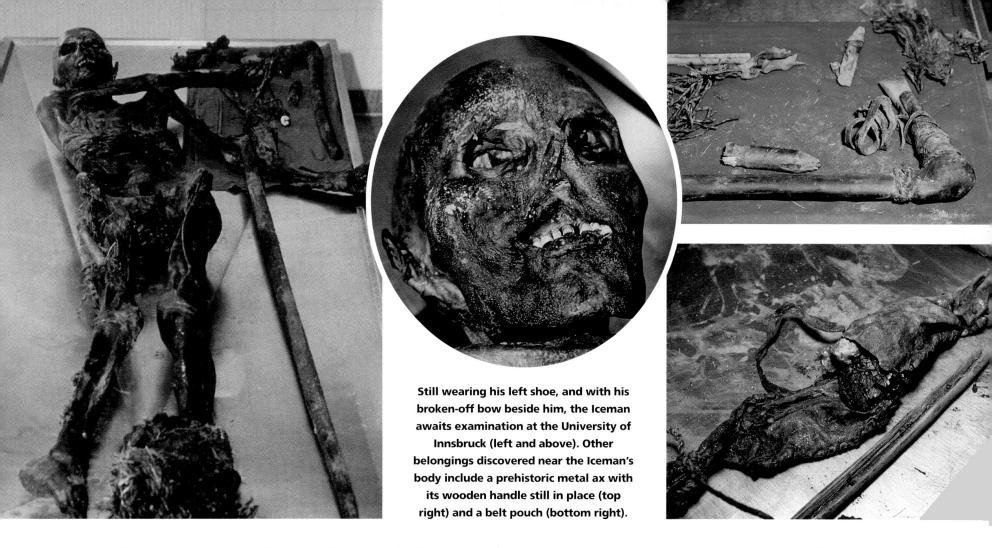

Still wearing his left shoe, and with his broken-off bow beside him, the Iceman awaits examination at the University of Innsbruck (left and above). Other belongings discovered near the Iceman's body include a prehistoric metal ax with its wooden handle still in place (top right) and a belt pouch (bottom right).

things that lay beside the body — the objects that had been found with the man. There was a long piece of wood that had been broken off at one end. There was a smooth, flat white bead attached to a fringe of tassels. There were odd-looking pieces of wood, rope, and leather. There was a pouch with a stone knife sticking out of it.

And there was an ax. It was small but well made. The handle had been carefully carved and shaped. The blade had been bound into the wood with leather straps.

Spindler's mind raced. He had seen axes like this before. He knew that such tools had been made only a very, very long time ago.

This was not the body of a mountain climber who had been dead for several decades — or even a warrior from the Middle Ages, as some people had guessed.

In fact, Konrad Spindler knew immediately that this man had died at least four thousand years ago.

It didn't take long for the news to spread. Suddenly, Spindler and the other researchers working on the body were bombarded with calls from journalists and curiosity-seekers. Photographs of the Iceman's face appeared on the front pages of newspapers all over the world. Scientists everywhere begged to study a piece of his body or his possessions.

People gave him nicknames. Some called him Frozen Fritz. Some called him Ötzi, after the Ötztal, the valley that lay north of where he was found.

Others wondered whether such an important discovery could even be real. They claimed that the Iceman was really a South American mummy that someone had planted in the ice as a joke.

Everyone wanted to see the body. Reporters and photographers instantly booked flights to Austria. The hot lights of their cameras began to damage some of the corpse's fragile tissues as they pressed in for a close look.

Postcards and T-shirts bearing the Iceman's

Why was the Iceman found intact?

1. About 5,300 years ago, the Iceman died in a narrow hollow in the mountains. Most likely a cold, dry snow began to fall shortly afterward, freeze-drying the body.

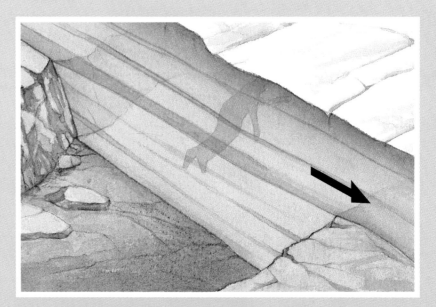

2. Over hundreds of years, more and more snow fell. Eventually a glacier moved over the rocks, but the Iceman's frozen body remained protected in the hollow underneath.

picture were sold. Candies were made in his shape. Songs were written about him. Books and TV specials were planned. Tour operators began offering guided hikes to the spot where he had been found.

Officials started to argue about who really owned the body. The Simons claimed that it was half theirs. Surveyors searched for the snow-covered border markers and learned that the body had actually been found in Italy. Would the Austrians have to give it back?

It was all very exciting. But meanwhile, behind the closed doors of the university, scientists and scholars were being called in. Already dozens of people had trampled over the discovery site, destroying valuable archeological evidence. Every person who had been near the spot where the body was found had to be tracked down and interviewed so archeologists could reconstruct the scene as exactly as possible. Further expeditions were planned to recover more objects. Every single item had to be preserved and cleaned —

3. Slowly the glacier began to melt. In 1991, desert storms in North Africa blew clouds of dust over the Alps. The dark dust absorbed the heat of the sun, causing the ice to melt more quickly.

4. In September 1991, Erika and Helmut Simon spotted the Iceman's head in the melting snow. Scientists believe the body had been uncovered for just three days before the discovery.

The Discovery Site

Many of the Iceman's belongings were found near his body. Pictured here are some of these artifacts as they would have looked during his life. Other remains included fragments of clothing and pieces of a wooden backpack frame.

Fur Hat

Archeologists found a fur hat during their second visit to the site in August 1992. It lay 28 inches (70 cm) from where the mummy's head had been.

Dagger

The Iceman carried a small dagger with a flint blade and a scabbard.

Quiver

A long fur sack made of deerskin, stiffened by a wooden rod, held the Iceman's fourteen arrows. Two of them were ready to use, with flint arrowheads still in place.

Bow

The Iceman had carefully placed his unfinished bow against a rock. It was broken in two during the recovery effort. The lower end of the bow was found stuck in the ice in August 1992.

Ax

The metal blade and shape of the ax head gave Konrad Spindler the first clue that the Iceman's body was at least four thousand years old.

Shoe

The Iceman's shoes were made from cowhide. Knotted grass cords formed a netting around the heel. The shoes were stuffed with grass for warmth.

Birch-bark Containers

Pieces of two birch-bark containers were found at the site; one of them had held embers for starting a fire.

What is carbon-14 dating?

Archeologists use carbon-14 dating to find out how old the remains of a plant, animal, or human are. Living things are made up of millions of tiny particles called atoms, and some of these are of a special kind called carbon 14. When a living thing dies, most of the atoms remain, but the carbon-14 atoms slowly begin to break down. By counting how many carbon-14 atoms were left in small pieces of the Iceman's bone and tissue, and in grass blades from his cape, scientists could tell that he died about 5,300 years ago.

a long, delicate job.

Experts identified the metal in the man's ax. They x-rayed his equipment. They tested his skin and bones and the grass found with him by a method known as carbon-14 dating.

Then all the tests were performed again, and the results were compared with those done by other scientists.

Finally there was no doubt. The body was even older than Konrad Spindler had guessed. The Iceman was 5,300 years old — his was the oldest human body that had ever been found so well preserved.

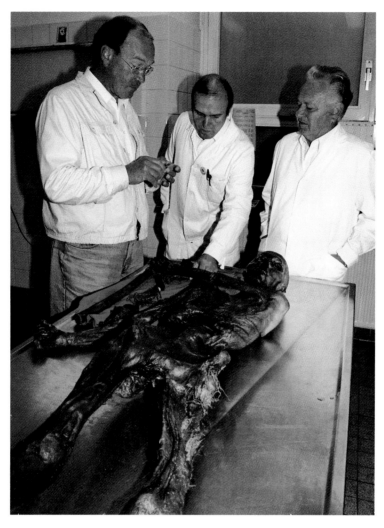

Archeologist Konrad Spindler (left) and other experts at the University of Innsbruck were amazed when test results proved that the Iceman was 5,300 years old.

The Iceman lived during the late Stone Age. He died five hundred years before the Egyptians built the first pyramids. He was already dead more than three thousand years before Jesus Christ was born.

For the archeologists, the real work was just beginning. There were hundreds of questions that needed to be answered.

What were all of the Iceman's belongings, and how had they been used? Could the long piece of wood really belong to a bow that had measured more than six feet (1.8 meters)? Why did it have no bowstring, and why were the arrows that the Iceman carried unfinished? What was the meaning of the flat white bead, and what could it have been used for? Why were a sour berry and pieces of animal bone found near the body? And why had he carried fresh maple leaves in a birch-bark container?

Who *was* the Iceman? What was he doing so high up on the mountain, and how did he die?

Part Two

THE ICEMAN'S STORY

How it might have been

The man bent down to pick up the basket of grain. As he reached for the handles, a gray dog pushed its cold, wet nose into his ear.

"Get away!" the man shouted, as precious grains of wheat spilled on the ground. "Or one day soon I will wring your neck and turn you into a good meal." But the man knew he wouldn't. The pesky dog had always been his youngest son's favorite.

The man began to gather up the spilled wheat. He straightened up slowly and tried to rub the soreness out of his lower back. He blinked the wheat dust out of his eyes.

"I can help." A tall lad with long black hair came over and took one handle. With the basket between them, they lugged the grain to the underground pit where it would be stored for the winter.

The teenager walked with long, easy strides. The older man tried to ignore his aching knees and struggled to keep up.

"Not so fast," he called out, his breath short. "These legs of mine are not so young anymore."

The boy nodded and smiled as he slowed his pace.

It had been a long day, but the man looked around now with satisfaction. The whole community had been working hard. They had cut and gathered the wheat. They had beaten the grains off the stalks. Now the wheat was neatly stored. If it could be kept dry and safe from rats, there should be enough to feed everyone until spring.

The man breathed in the sharp scent of freshly cut straw and the faint swampy smell coming from the river. The soil in the valley was rich, and the harvest had been good this year. They had plenty of grain, and there was a good supply of barley and peas. The cattle were healthy. And soon the men of the village would head into the forests to hunt for wild boar and red deer. The man was looking forward to bringing back something big this year. When his new longbow was finished, it would be powerful enough to take down a giant wild aurochs with one well-placed shot.

A crowd of children came running around the side of the barn. They screamed with laughter as they pelted one another with armfuls of straw. They were supposed to be gathering it to use as bedding for the animals. Instead they seemed to be scattering it all over the village.

The man said nothing. The children had been working as hard as the adults. They should enjoy the warm evenings while they lasted. All too soon the valley would be covered with a blanket of fog and snow.

The children thundered past him, flinging straw as they went. The man looked for his own seven-year-old son, the youngest of his four children. The boy was usually at the head of the pack. Why wasn't he with the others now?

The man climbed the hill to his home. Although it was early evening, there was still plenty of activity. The villagers were using every minute of daylight

Piecing Together the Iceman's Life

All kinds of clues have helped to piece together a picture of who the Iceman was and what his life was like.

Kernels of Grain

Two barleycorns, in their husks, were caught in the fur tufts of the Iceman's clothing. The remains of wheat were found in one of his birch-bark containers. These suggest that he had recently been in a village where grain was being harvested.

What Bones and Teeth Tell Us

Scientists examined the Iceman's skull and teeth to discover how old he was when he died. Skull bones grow more closely together as a person ages, and teeth wear down from chewing. The Iceman's teeth are very worn, perhaps from chewing animal hides to soften them or from chewing sand — sand was often accidentally mixed with the wheat when it was ground into flour. From the evidence of his skull and teeth, archeologists estimate that the Iceman was between 25 and 40 years old.

Traces of Copper

Large amounts of copper have been found on the surface of the Iceman's hair. Scientists are now investigating his fingers and lungs. If a lot of copper is found there, too, it is possible that the Iceman spent much of his time melting down copper to make tools. Or he may have simply spent a lot of time sharpening and polishing his ax.

Hunting and Gathering

The Iceman probably hunted wild boar (top), ibex (middle), hare (below), and red deer (bottom), as well as bears, birds and the now-extinct aurochs — large, long-horned wild oxen. He used as much of an animal as he could — meat for food, skins for clothing, antler and bone for tools, sinew for sewing and to make tools and bowstrings, and feathers for the ends of arrows.

Villagers supplemented their food supply with crab apples, berries, acorns, and hazelnuts.

before the sun dropped down behind the mountains. Some were grinding grain into flour. Others sharpened their axes and knives. Still others were using stone tools to scrape the flesh off animal hides.

People waved as the man passed. The mood was light. Autumn was a time of hard work, but there was reason to celebrate, too. There would be two marriages in the village this fall, and feasting for the entire valley.

"Father, look!" The man's younger daughter stood outside the house. She was carrying a large bowl filled with nuts.

"Acorns for flour," she said proudly. "I gathered them myself."

"You've done well," the man said, picking up a plump nut and breaking it open with his teeth. "But look. These acorns are from the red oak. They will be bitter. The white acorns are better."

His daughter scowled as she carried her basket around to the back of the house. The man smiled. She was growing into a fine young woman, but she was only twelve years old. She still had a great deal to learn.

Inside the house, it was unusually quiet. The fire was untended. On the bed lay his youngest son. The boy's mother sat beside him.

"Our boy is sick," she said to her husband. "My aunt is coming to see him."

His wife's aunt was the oldest woman in the valley. She knew how to make medicines from herbs and mushrooms that she gathered in the woods. The man himself had gone to her for the aches in his legs and back. She had made healing marks on his skin, but they had not yet helped.

The man walked over to the bed. His son lay on his side. The boy's knees were pulled up to his belly in pain.

The man looked at his wife, and he could see his own worry reflected in her eyes. They had both seen this illness before. The tiny unmarked grave outside the house was a reminder of the last time such a sickness had swept through the village.

The man's wife drew a blanket over the little boy. "Have our other children returned?" she asked.

He shook his head. A small group of young people, including their eldest son and daughter, had been up in the mountains since spring. They had been caring for the village goat herd in the high pastures. They usually returned home in good time to help with the harvest, but not this season. Clouds had ringed the mountains for several days. If the young people were caught by the first snows, they would have trouble making their way home before winter.

Ancient Cures

The Iceman has given us some ideas about how illnesses were treated more than five thousand years ago. Blue tattoos, probably made with charcoal, were found on the Iceman's back (left), knee, leg, feet, and ankles. X-rays show that his joints were becoming weak in almost all of these

areas due to old age and strain. The tattooing may have been done as a form of folk medicine to relieve the pain in his joints.

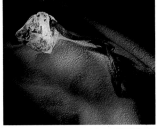

Found among the Iceman's belongings were pieces of birch-tree fungus threaded onto narrow strips of fur (right). This fungus has been used as a medicine since ancient times because it contains an antibiotic that can fight off illness.

The Grass Cloak and Fur Hat

The Iceman wore a long cloak made from plaited grass, which kept off the rain. Pieces of the cloak (above) were found beneath his body. The back part of the cloak was missing, perhaps blown away once the body was free from the ice. The fur hat (left) is the oldest of its kind ever seen in Europe.

"Where are you going?" The twelve-year-old watched her father fill his backpack.

"The elders have agreed that I should go to look for your brother and sister and the others," he told his daughter.

"But your legs hurt. You are slow. How can you climb the mountain?"

"Don't forget that I also tended the herd when I was a boy. I know the paths and summer camps better than anyone. Perhaps that will make up for my slowness."

"How long will you be gone?"

"Several days. After I find your sister and brother, I will stop to hunt in the next valley. Red deer often come down to drink at the creek there when the cold weather comes."

The girl looked at her father's half-carved bow and mostly unfinished arrows. They lay in a neat row on the ground.

"You only have two real arrows," she said doubtfully.

The man laughed. "I will have time to make more," he said. "These old legs of mine cannot climb all day long. When I stop to rest, I will sharpen and carve. Now, bring me those fur clothes you have been mending for me. It will be cold in the mountains."

His daughter bit her lip and stood up. She headed slowly toward the house.

"Don't let that beast inside," he warned, as the gray dog trotted behind her hopefully.

When the girl reappeared, her arms were filled with clothing. She handed her father his fur tunic, fur hat, and heavy grass raincloak. She did not look at him as he examined her mending job. She knew her stitches were clumsy, and she had used crude grass thread instead of sinew. The man shook his head. "It will be some time before you are as skilled a sewer as your mother," he said. "But you will only learn with practice."

"He's no better?" the man asked his wife. She shook her head. The boy lay with his head in her lap. His mother was holding a necklace made of a flat white bead with a fringe of twisted leather. As she rocked the boy, she held the bead in her hand and gently rubbed his stomach.

The old aunt kneeled beside the fire. She was cutting up birch fungus and dropping it into a steaming broth. "Three others in the village have the same sickness," she said. "They drank water from down the river, close to where the cattle have been

Sharpening Flint Blades

Flint, a very hard stone used to make sharp blades and arrowheads, was precious in prehistoric times. The flint the Iceman carried may have come from deposits in Italy, south of the Alps.

At first archeologists were puzzled by this antler-tipped tool (top right), but experts believe it was used for shaping and sharpening fine flint blades such as the one on the dagger (bottom right). The cutting edge was sharpened by pressing off small shell-shaped flakes of flint with the retouching tool (above).

23

wading." She took two pieces of dried fungus and laced them onto a strip of fur. She handed it to the man. "Medicine. In case you need it."

The man took the medicine. He turned to go.

"Wait." His wife laid the boy's head down gently. She stood up and walked over to the door. Her lips were cracked and dry. The man wondered whether she might have the sickness, too.

"Take this." She pressed the necklace into his hand. "May the spirits help you find our children and return safely."

The man nodded. He went outside. As he was about to close the door, a hard muzzle bumped up against his hand.

The man looked back at his sick son. He pushed the door open a little and the dog nosed its way inside. It bounded over to the boy and licked his face. The man saw his son open his eyes and reach for the animal.

The man pulled on his pack and quiver. He gathered up his bow and ax. Then he began to follow the river up into the mountains.

Charms and Spirits

The Iceman may have worn this fur tassel with a polished marble bead (left) as a good-luck charm.

Many ancient people believed in gods or spirits, and picture stones like this one (right) may have been sacred to them. Engraved with pictures of weapons and axes, this seven-foot (two-meter) stone was found in Italy.

Making a Fire

One of the Iceman's birch-bark containers was blackened on the inside. It was used for carrying embers, or pieces of charcoal, which were wrapped in maple leaves and covered with wet grasses (diagram below). When the Iceman needed to make a fire, he would remove the embers, add tinder, and blow (above). Archeologists have pieced together the fragile remains of one of the containers (left). Flakes of charcoal can still be seen on the ancient maple leaves (bottom left).

Dusk came early on this part of the mountain. The man watched as the sun dropped behind the ridge. He took a couple of green maple leaves from his birch-bark container and unwrapped embers to start a fire. He made some barley porridge, mixing it on a flat stone. He had been unable to catch a bird or hare for his evening meal.

Later, the man worked on his bow, shaving off thin flakes with his ax. He ran his hands over the tough yet supple wood. It had taken him a long time to find this perfect piece of yew. Now the bow was almost finished. Once the string was firmly attached, it would make a powerful weapon. No need to be fast on your feet when you had a bow like this. A strong arm and a keen eye were enough to fell a deer thirty paces away.

The man took a deep breath. The cold caught in his lungs. He coughed and shivered.

He had been walking for days now, and the nights were getting colder. But he had not yet found the young people. He had checked the summer camp, but it had been abandoned long ago.

Then why hadn't they arrived home? Why hadn't he met them on the path?

The Iceman's Bow and Arrows

Made from strong, flexible yew wood, the Iceman's bow (left and right) was nearly six feet (two meters) long. When it was finished, the bow would have been powerful enough to hunt large game such as deer and ibex.

Two finished arrows were found in the deerskin quiver (below), along with twelve arrow shafts, a stag-antler spike used as an all-purpose tool, and a cord, possibly for the bowstring (above). To complete the arrows, the Iceman would have inserted a flint arrowhead into each shaft, glued it with birch tar, and wrapped it tightly with animal sinew. He would then attach feathers to the end of each shaft, cementing them with birch tar (left). The angle of the feathers made the arrows spin as they flew, for truer aim.

A long, cool howl split the dusk.

The sound came straight from the ridge like an arrow. It was a wolf, the swiftest, strongest hunter in the land.

The wolf howled again. The man opened his arms to the sound. If he let the spirit of the wolf enter into him, maybe he would share some of its hunting skill.

Another wail joined the first one, and then another. Soon there was a whole chorus of howls, some high and piercing, some low and quivering.

The man frowned. When the wolves sang together, it meant the first snows were not far behind. He would start off again at dawn. He must find the young people soon.

The man slowly made his way up the mountain. The path was steep and littered with fallen rocks. Had the young people been caught in a rock slide? The man knew how swiftly a piece of the mountain could come rushing down the slope, breaking apart and instantly burying everything in its path.

For a moment the man thought he heard voices. He stopped to listen. A cool rush of mountain air came at him, but it contained nothing. He listened once more. A faint whistling sound floated over the ridge.

A thrush? Still in the mountains so close to winter?

The man headed in the direction of the whistling. He heard it again, a throaty trill.

He walked more quickly, his spirits rising. He knew that sound. It was the special call his daughter used to summon the goats.

Alpine Wolves

Roving packs of wolves in the mountains once presented a serious threat to shepherds' flocks. Although they were common in the Iceman's day, wolves are now rarely seen in Europe.

"Father!" A noisy group of young people, dogs, and goats came bounding over the ridge — his son, his daughter, and their two cousins, all surrounded by a flurry of yapping, braying beasts.

The man smiled as he counted everyone safe. He had found them.

They made their camp early that evening. The young people told the man that the wolves had circled the herd and scattered the goats all over the western flank of the mountain. It had taken them many days to round them up and begin heading back to the main track.

The man was happy to let the young people gather wood and prepare the fire. He lent his son his ax and watched him cut down saplings with skill.

They roasted part of an ibex that his son had killed. The man watched the young people eating heartily, wrestling with the dogs, and flinging bones into the fire.

He looked down at his ax. He ran a finger along

Summer Herding in Mountain Pastures

Once people began to farm and keep livestock, they had to settle in one place so that they could provide shelter and food for their animals in winter. But each summer, animal herders would take sheep and goats up to high mountain pastures for months at a time. This practice is still common in the Alpine region today. Shepherds drive their flocks from the valleys south of the Alps up across the same mountain passes that the Iceman would have traveled.

How was his copper ax made?

At first archeologist Konrad Spindler thought the Iceman's ax (above) was four thousand years old. This was the time when tools were made of bronze, an alloy of copper and tin. But carbon-14 dating showed that the mummy was 5,300 years old, from an era long before bronze tools were made. A study of the metal in the ax proved that it was almost pure copper.

To melt copper, early metalworkers used blowpipes, fanning the fire until it reached at least 2,226°F (1,100°C). The copper was then poured into an upright mold made of sandstone or clay.

The Iceman's ax was made from a strong piece of yew wood with a branch sticking out at a right angle for the handle. The blade had been cemented in place with birch tar and wrapped with narrow strips of leather.

Ancient people often were buried with valuable possessions such as this.

the blade. Cutting wood always blunted the edge very quickly. It needed to be sharpened, but it was still a fine tool. The man had hoped to have it buried with him, but perhaps he would give it to his son instead.

His elder daughter sat beside him. She was watching her father intently. A sudden shift in the breeze blew smoke in their direction. The man began to cough, but the cough came from deep in his chest, and he couldn't seem to stop. He wiped his eyes and spat on the ground.

"Come home with us in the morning, Father," she begged. "There is plenty of time for hunting. Come back to the village."

The girl had eyes like a fox. She noticed everything. The man knew she had been watching his slow, painful movements. She saw his unfinished bow,

the small amount of barley in his pack, his empty net bag.

Her sharp gaze annoyed him.

"No," he said firmly. "These cold nights will bring the deer down to the creek bed in the next valley." He looked at the girl's anxious face. "Don't worry. I will be home in time for the harvest feast."

The next morning the man said good-bye to the young people. He waved, smiling at their high spirits as they herded the goats down the craggy slopes.

The man picked up his pack. As he did, he noticed that someone had placed a large piece of meat and some berries inside. He inspected a handful of the berries. They were bitter and tasteless. He flung them away in disgust.

At midday he stopped to rest. Thin clouds had settled over the mountain, but the pale orb of the sun gleamed dully through the haze. He cut some grass and stuffed it into his shoes for warmth. He didn't eat. His stomach hurt. He dozed.

When he opened his eyes, the world was transformed. Fog was creeping up the slope, its white mist reaching for his skin like damp fingers.

He gathered his things hurriedly and headed uphill. He must climb higher, to where the cold, dry winds would blow away the fog.

The going was slow. The path was narrow and rough. There were no saplings or bushes to grab on to. The man used his bow as a walking stick,

A sloe berry provides a clue...

A single sloe berry found with the Iceman suggests that he died in the early fall, when sloe berries (right) ripen. (Sloe berries are too bitter to eat until after the first frost, and even then they can be quite sour.) A study of the pollen in the glacier where the Iceman was found also shows that he died in late summer or early fall.

but the fog seemed to stay only steps behind him.

He paused and gasped. The air was thin so high up, and it was hard to breathe. It was very cold. He could not go farther without rest.

Ahead of him lay a little hollow that sloped down to a small rock face. He would stop here for the night.

The man made his way into the hollow, slipping a bit on the damp stone. He leaned his pack, bow, and ax against a nearby rock and sat down. His stomach ached.

He wasn't sure how long he had dozed when he next opened his eyes. He felt strangely warm. He took off his fur hat. He knew he should make a broth with the aunt's medicine, but he was too tired to make a fire.

He lay down. For a while he held his wife's necklace close to his chest. He wondered whether his son and daughter had arrived home safely.

A light snow began to fall. It covered his hair and his face, but it felt soft and warm. The man rolled onto his side. The necklace fell out of his hand.

It was very quiet, very still. But as the man fell into sleep, he heard familiar sounds through the muffled blanket of snow.

The wolf pack had begun to sing again.

Part Three
THE ICEMAN AND US

Nobody knows for certain where the Iceman came from, or exactly how he died. He could have been a shepherd who was caught in a sudden snowstorm while bringing his herd down the mountain. He could have been hunting animals or looking for precious metals on the rocky mountain slopes. He could have been fleeing an enemy attack on his village. Maybe he was a religious leader who had gone up to the mountains to pray. Or perhaps he was just on his way to visit friends in a hilltop village.

The Iceman may not even have died alone. He could have been with other people. His friends may have survived and returned to their homes, or their bodies may have been ground up by the glacier. Or they may still lie under the ice, waiting to be discovered.

Already more than one hundred scientists from seven countries, have studied the Iceman, including Konrad Spindler. Plant specialists have examined the berry and maple leaves found near the body and the grass from the Iceman's cloak and shoes. Animal specialists have studied his leather clothes and the pieces of ibex bone that were found near him. Rock and metal experts have examined the copper blade of his ax and the stone in his tools. Archeologists are carefully cleaning and piecing together more than one hundred torn and crushed scraps of leather to reconstruct the Iceman's clothing. Others have made copies of his ax and bow, with exactly the same tools and materials, to see how they were made and used.

Doctors have examined the Iceman's lungs, bones, and hair. They have learned that he had unhealthy lungs and an injured back, neck, and legs. He also had a parasite in his intestines that may have made him sick.

It will take many years before experts find out

Fragile Remains

The crude way in which the Iceman and his belongings were removed from the ice damaged both the body and several precious artifacts. By the time archeologists reached the site, it was too late to make an accurate record of where everything had been found. Specialists had to sort through a jumbled pile of belongings (left) and piece together clothing from scraps of leather (above). The Iceman still wore the remains of one shoe, stuffed with grass, but only the inner netting of the other shoe has survived (below).

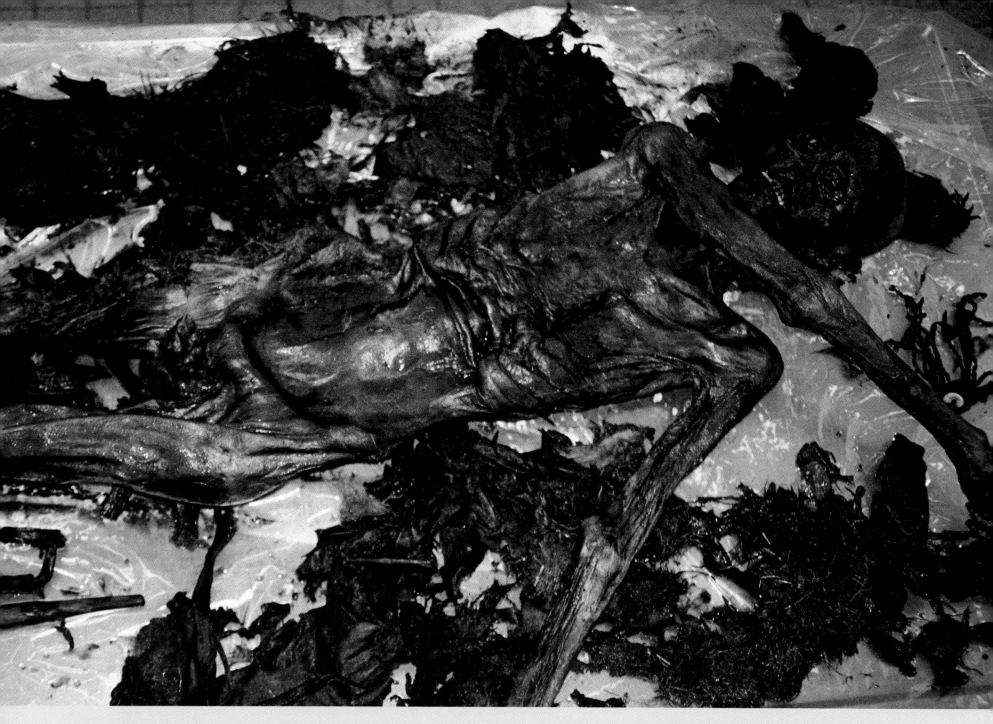

The Iceman's body shrank as it dried out, so scientists measured the length of his thighbone to help them estimate his height before he died. Based on their calculations, the Iceman stood five feet three inches (160 cm) tall. He is now bald, but hairs found among his clothing show that he had wavy dark brown hair at least three inches (9 cm) long, and he probably had a beard. A small depression in his right earlobe suggests that he also may have worn an earring.

everything they can about the Iceman. Scientists still want to examine his stomach and internal organs to find out what he ate or what illnesses he had. They will try to learn things about his immune system that may help us understand diseases today.

This is all slow, detailed work. It takes money and sophisticated equipment to do these complicated tests. Results must be checked and double-checked. It also takes time for scientists to share their information with the rest of the world so their results can be studied by other experts.

And the work is just beginning. Many years from now, a whole new generation of young archeologists will still be piecing together the thousands of clues that the Iceman has left us.

Meanwhile, the Iceman is locked in a special freezer at the University of Innsbruck. He is sandwiched between layers of surgical gauze, crushed ice, and plastic wrap. His body is kept at the same humidity and temperature as the glacier. When he is removed from the freezer,

everyone must wear surgical gowns, masks, and gloves. He can be examined for only thirty minutes at a time. After that, his body will start to rot. Once he is back in his freezer, it takes two full days before he returns to his frozen temperature.

Even with this special care (it costs $10,000 a month just to keep the Iceman), his body is drying out. As one scientist said, he now looks "like a slab of meat that's been in the freezer too long."

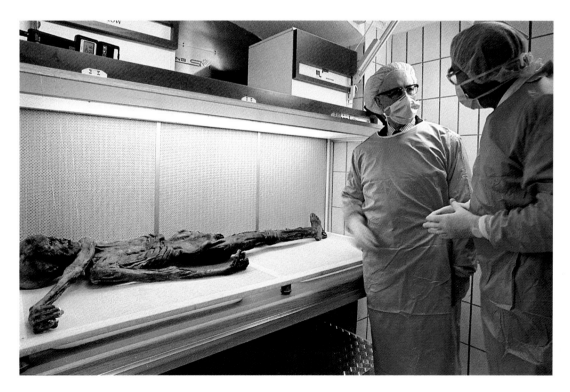

Dressed like surgeons in a hospital operating room, scientists study the Iceman for brief periods. Afterward the body is carefully refrozen. This will preserve it for study in future years when scientific techniques will be more advanced than they are today.

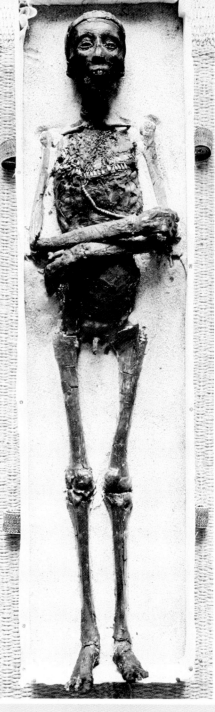

What Mummies Tell Us

Because the Iceman died suddenly and was not formally buried, he reveals more about everyday life in his time than a mummy found in a grave. But all mummies have fascinating stories to tell.

This sand-dried body from Egypt (above) was buried, surrounded by pots of food and necklaces, in a shallow grave about five thousand years ago. Later, the Egyptians began to embalm their dead. The mummy of Tutankhamun (right) is one of the most famous ever found and is more than three thousand years old. The fabulous discovery of Tutankhamun's tomb in 1922 revealed stunning treasures, meant to provide for the boy-king in his afterlife.

In 1995, the five-hundred-year-old mummy of a frozen Inca girl (opposite, bottom), believed to have been killed as a human sacrifice, was found in the mountains of Peru. Scientists plan to study her internal organs to learn more about what Inca people ate and how healthy they were.

Another sacrifice victim was found preserved in a peat bog in Denmark in 1950, his leather cap still in place (opposite, top). Known as Tollund man, he is more than two thousand years old.

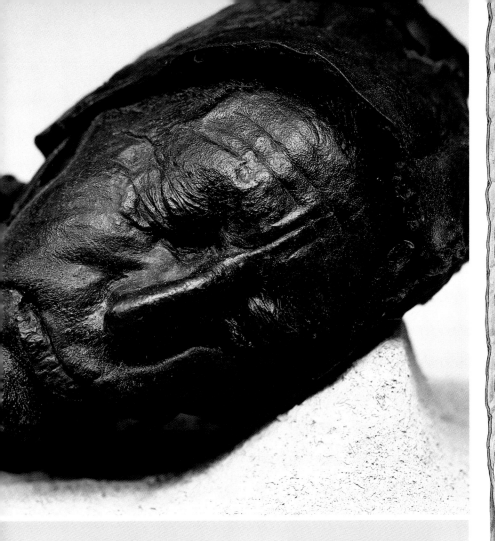

Recent carbon dating found that the Spirit Cave man, a mummy discovered in Nevada in the 1940s, is more than 9,400 years old, making him the oldest known mummy in North America. The skin of his head and one shoulder were preserved by the dry environment of the cave in which he was found. He had been wrapped in shrouds woven from marsh plants and was wearing moccasins.

In the meantime, officials are still arguing about how the body should be treated. How much of the Iceman should be cut up and given to scientists to study? Should he be put in a glass case and displayed in a museum? To whom does he belong?

And even when all these things are sorted out, we may still never know exactly who the Iceman was.

So why should we care about him? What can he tell us?

Finding old bodies is nothing new. Over the years, archeologists have discovered pieces of skeleton fossils in Africa that belonged to our earliest human ancestors who lived about four million years ago. They have opened graves containing the mummies of Egyptian kings. In those the brains and internal organs have been removed, and the bodies have been preserved by embalming. They have dug up hundred-year-old corpses buried in the frozen Canadian Arctic. And in the peat bogs of northern Europe they have found the bodies of sacrifice victims who lived more than two thousand years ago.

But the Iceman is the oldest complete body ever found. Not only that, he was not found in a grave. Bodies in graves have often been cleaned up or specially dressed or arranged. They are often buried with articles that may or may not have belonged to

One of the most important archeological discoveries of this century, the Iceman has greatly expanded our knowledge of life in the late Stone Age.

them — articles that are meant to be used in the afterlife.

The Iceman died as he was going about the business of his everyday life. He was wearing his regular clothes, carrying his everyday tools. It's as if he has just walked out of a time machine that has traveled through 5,300 years into the present. By studying him, we can learn a great deal about the daily life of our ancestors.

Long before the Iceman lived, humans were hunters and gatherers. They followed the herds and animals that they caught and ate. They moved from place to place as different food plants ripened. They had only the belongings that they could carry on their backs.

Accidents were common, and often more children died than lived. But in general, people existed peaceably, living and dying according to the cycles of the natural world.

By the time the Iceman was born, people had begun to farm and to settle in one place. They grew food that could be stored so they could survive the winters without starving. Although they still hunted wild animals, they also kept cows, goats, and pigs. They built homes and formed villages. They mined different kinds of metals and stone, made pottery, and created new tools for farming.

More children were born, and more lived to become adults. In a farming community, larger families were useful. Even very young children could help with jobs such as gathering nuts and hauling wood and water.

But living in one place did not mean that life was always easy. People could grow their own food, but dry weather, insects, floods, or an early frost could wipe out a whole season's harvest. When people and animals lived close together and used the same water, disease could quickly spread. Villages might raid one another for food or goods.

Like their ancestors, people remained closely linked to the natural world. They kept track of time by watching the changing seasons and the position of the sun and the moon. They knew which soils were good for farming, where the best places were for animals to graze. They knew exactly what kind of wood

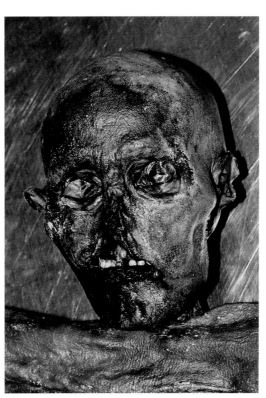

would make the best backpack frame, bow, or ax handle. They knew the best time to pick berries and nuts. They used plants for food and medicine. They knew how to use every part of an animal for food, tools, and clothing.

There was more to the Iceman's life than work and survival. He probably had a family that he cared for. He may have believed in gods or spirits. He and his people likely found time to celebrate special events like births, marriages, and a good harvest. They exchanged ideas and goods with villages close by and far away.

When we look at photographs of the Iceman, we see a shriveled, naked body and a battered, sunken face. But that body and face belonged to a real human being. They belonged to a man who lived in a world that was probably inhabited by people just like him — people who were in many ways not so different from ourselves.

The Iceman's Place in Time

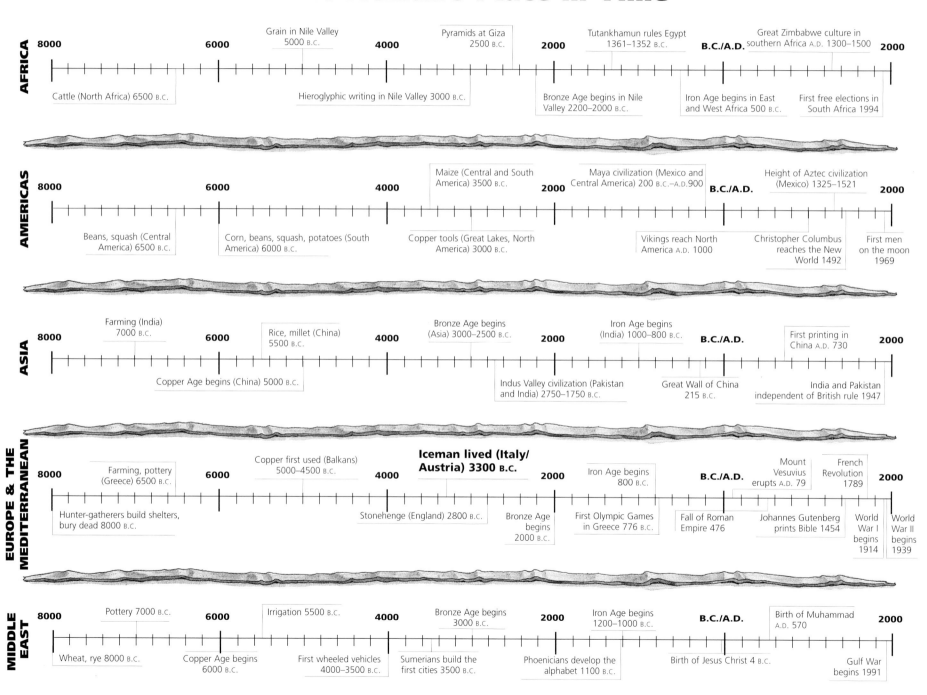

AFRICA

8000 — 6000 — 4000 — 2000 — B.C./A.D. — 2000

Grain in Nile Valley 5000 B.C. · Pyramids at Giza 2500 B.C. · Tutankhamun rules Egypt 1361–1352 B.C. · Great Zimbabwe culture in southern Africa A.D. 1300–1500

Cattle (North Africa) 6500 B.C. · Hieroglyphic writing in Nile Valley 3000 B.C. · Bronze Age begins in Nile Valley 2200–2000 B.C. · Iron Age begins in East and West Africa 500 B.C. · First free elections in South Africa 1994

AMERICAS

8000 — 6000 — 4000 — 2000 — B.C./A.D. — 2000

Maize (Central and South America) 3500 B.C. · Maya civilization (Mexico and Central America) 200 B.C.–A.D. 900 · Height of Aztec civilization (Mexico) 1325–1521

Beans, squash (Central America) 6500 B.C. · Corn, beans, squash, potatoes (South America) 6000 B.C. · Copper tools (Great Lakes, North America) 3000 B.C. · Vikings reach North America A.D. 1000 · Christopher Columbus reaches the New World 1492 · First men on the moon 1969

ASIA

8000 — 6000 — 4000 — 2000 — B.C./A.D. — 2000

Farming (India) 7000 B.C. · Rice, millet (China) 5500 B.C. · Bronze Age begins (Asia) 3000–2500 B.C. · Iron Age begins (India) 1000–800 B.C. · First printing in China A.D. 730

Copper Age begins (China) 5000 B.C. · Indus Valley civilization (Pakistan and India) 2750–1750 B.C. · Great Wall of China 215 B.C. · India and Pakistan independent of British rule 1947

EUROPE & THE MEDITERRANEAN

8000 — 6000 — 4000 — 2000 — B.C./A.D. — 2000

Copper first used (Balkans) 5000–4500 B.C. · **Iceman lived (Italy/Austria) 3300 B.C.** · Iron Age begins 800 B.C. · Mount Vesuvius erupts A.D. 79 · French Revolution 1789

Farming, pottery (Greece) 6500 B.C. · Hunter-gatherers build shelters, bury dead 8000 B.C. · Stonehenge (England) 2800 B.C. · Bronze Age begins 2000 B.C. · First Olympic Games in Greece 776 B.C. · Fall of Roman Empire 476 · Johannes Gutenberg prints Bible 1454 · World War I begins 1914 · World War II begins 1939

MIDDLE EAST

8000 — 6000 — 4000 — 2000 — B.C./A.D. — 2000

Pottery 7000 B.C. · Irrigation 5500 B.C. · Bronze Age begins 3000 B.C. · Iron Age begins 1200–1000 B.C. · Birth of Muhammad A.D. 570

Wheat, rye 8000 B.C. · Copper Age begins 6000 B.C. · First wheeled vehicles 4000–3500 B.C. · Sumerians build the first cities 3500 B.C. · Phoenicians develop the alphabet 1100 B.C. · Birth of Jesus Christ 4 B.C. · Gulf War begins 1991

Glossary

alloy: A mixture of two or more elements, at least one of which is a metal.

Alps: A range of mountains in Europe that stretches across parts of France, Switzerland, Italy, and Austria.

archeologist: A person who studies people from the past and their cultures.

artifact: An object made by people of an ancient or prehistoric culture.

aurochs: A large, long-horned wild ox that lived in Europe but is now extinct. The aurochs was the ancestor of modern-day domestic cattle.

birch fungus: An organism that grows on birch trees and contains an antibiotic that can fight off infection.

corpse: A dead human body.

crevasse: A deep, open crack in a glacier.

embalm: To treat a dead body so that it will not decay.

ember: A small glowing fragment of coal or charcoal from a fire.

forensic expert: A person who uses scientific techniques to investigate a question, especially a crime, relating to the law.

ibex: A wild goat, with curved ridged horns, found in the mountains of Europe, North Africa, and Asia.

Middle Ages: The period of European history from about A.D. 500 to 1500.

mummy: The body of a person or animal that has been preserved by some process that stops decay, such as drying, freezing, or complete water saturation.

parasite: An organism that lives in or on a host organism, usually causing it harm.

peat bog: Wet, spongy ground where plants have partially broken down forming a brown deposit like soil.

prehistoric: From a time before written records.

quiver: A case for carrying arrows.

scabbard: A sheath or case for a dagger or sword.

sinew: A strand of tough, fiberlike tissue that attaches a muscle to a bone. Once dried and twisted, animal sinew could be made into a strong thread for sewing clothes or making tools.

Stone Age: The prehistoric period when most tools and weapons were made from stone.

summit: The highest point of a mountain.

yew: A kind of evergreen tree or shrub with sturdy wood, used for centuries to make bows.

PICTURE CREDITS

All illustrations are by Laurie McGaw unless otherwise stated.

Front cover: (Top left) Sygma (Bottom left) Paul Hanny/ Gamma/Ponopresse Internationale Inc. (Top right) Rex Features London/Ponopresse Internationale Inc. (Bottom right) G. Hinter-leitner/Gamma/ Ponopresse Internationale Inc.

Back cover: (Diagram) Jack McMaster (Middle) Kenneth Garrett/National Geographic Image Collection (Bottom) Rex Features London/ Ponopresse Internationale Inc.

Front flap: Werner Nosko/ © SNS Pressebild

Endpapers: Jakob Tappeiner

4: (Middle) Erika and Helmut Simon (Thong motif) Jack McMaster

5: (Top) Jakob Tappeiner (Inset) Erika and Helmut Simon (Map) Jack McMaster

6: (Diagram) Jack McMaster (Top) Paul Hanny/ Gamma/Ponopresse Internationale Inc.

7: Anton Koler/ Forschungsinstitut für Alpine Vorzeit, Universität Innsbruck

8: (Top) Sygma (Middle and bottom) Rex Features London/Ponopresse Internationale Inc.

9: (Left, middle, and top right) Sygma (Bottom right) G. Hinterleitner/ Gamma/Ponopresse Internationale Inc.

10-11: (Diagrams) Jack McMaster

12: (Diagram) Jack McMaster

13: Werner Nosko/© SNS Pressebild

18: Animals Animals © Robert Maier

20: (Left) Paul Hanny/ Gamma/Ponopresse Internationale Inc. (Right) Kenneth Garrett/National Geographic Image Collection

22: (Top) Kenneth Garrett/National Geographic Image Collection (Bottom) Walter Leitner/ Forschungsinstitut für Alpine Vorzeit, Universität Innsbruck

23: (Diagram) Jack McMaster (Top and bottom) Kenneth Garrett/National Geographic Image Collection

24: Kenneth Garrett/National Geographic Image Collection

26: (Diagrams) Jack McMaster (Middle) Walter Leitner/ Forschungsinstitut für Alpine Vorzeit, Universität Innsbruck (Bottom) Klaus Oeggl/Forschungsinstitut für Alpine Vorzeit, Universität Innsbruck

27: (Diagrams) Jack McMaster (Top) Copyright: Römisch-Germanisches Zentralmuseum (Christin Beeck) (Bottom) Kenneth Garrett/National Geographic Image Collection

28: Animals Animals © Peter Weimann

30: (Left) Animals Animals © Sydney Thomson (Right) Kenneth Garrett/National Geographic Image Collection

32: (Top) Kenneth Garrett/National Geographic Image Collection (Diagram) Jack McMaster

34: Photo Researchers, Inc. © Anton Thielemann/ OKAPIA

39: (Left) Sygma (Top right) Kenneth Garrett/National Geographic Image Collection (Bottom right) Copyright: Römisch-Germanisches Zentralmuseum (Christin Beeck)

40: Rex Features London/Ponopresse Internationale Inc.

41: Kenneth Garrett/National Geographic Image Collection

42: (Left) Copyright British Museum (Right) The Griffith Institute

43: (Top) Silkeborg Museum, Denmark (Bottom) Johan Reinhard

44: (Left and inset) Rex Features London/Ponopresse Internationale Inc.

45: Werner Nosko/©SNS Pressebild

RECOMMENDED FURTHER READING

FROZEN MAN
by David Getz, illustrated by Peter McCarty
(Henry Holt and Company, U.S. and Canada)

A fascinating account of the discovery of the Iceman and how scientists are using clues to piece together a picture of his life.

THE ICEMAN
by Don Lessem
(Crown Publishers, Inc., U.S. and Canada)

Written for younger readers, this story also relates the thrilling discovery of the 5,300-year-old Iceman in the Alps.

THE MAN IN THE ICE
by Konrad Spindler
(Harmony Books, U.S.; C. Bertelsman, Verlag, Germany; Weidenfeld and Nicholson, U.K.)

An in-depth account of the discovery and excavation of the Iceman by the chief archeologist involved in the research project and a team of international scientists. Includes detailed descriptions of the mummy, the clothing and equipment found with him, and life in the Alpine area in the late Stone Age.

ACKNOWLEDGMENTS

Laurie McGaw would like to extend special thanks to Peter Muir, who posed (good-naturedly) for the Iceman. Thanks also to the following friends who took time to pose for all the other villagers: Bruce Barnes, Jessie Cooper-Barnes, Thomas Cooper-Barnes, Janet Coulter, Amy Galbraith, Daryl Galbraith, Jill Galbraith, Justin Galbraith, Ryan Galbraith, Stephanie Galbraith, Denise Gale, Lian Goodall, Barry Hebden, Lynnette Hebden, Mary Ann Hutchings, Laurie May, Katelyn Mansell, Michael Meunier, Alison Lyle-Moutrey, Laura Moutrey, Nicholas Moutrey, Paul Panagiotou, Gwynne Phillips, Miranda Pylypink, Christina Scavone, and Steve Stewart.

Madison Press Books would like to thank Heinz Müller, Sabina Seeber-Kneußl, and Julia Stadler of the University of Innsbruck; John Provan; Dr. G. Waurick of the Römisch-Germanisches Zentralmuseum; and Alison Reid.